SOCCER

Written by Brad Herzog

Table of Contents

Introduction 2
Where Did Soccer Come From? . . 6
How Do You Play? 8
What Is the World Cup? 14
Who Is the Best Ever? 18

Celebration Press
An Imprint of ScottForesman

Introduction

What is the most popular sport in the world? Do you think it might be basketball? Or baseball? Or hockey? In fact, it is a sport that most of the world calls "football." In the United States, it is known as soccer.

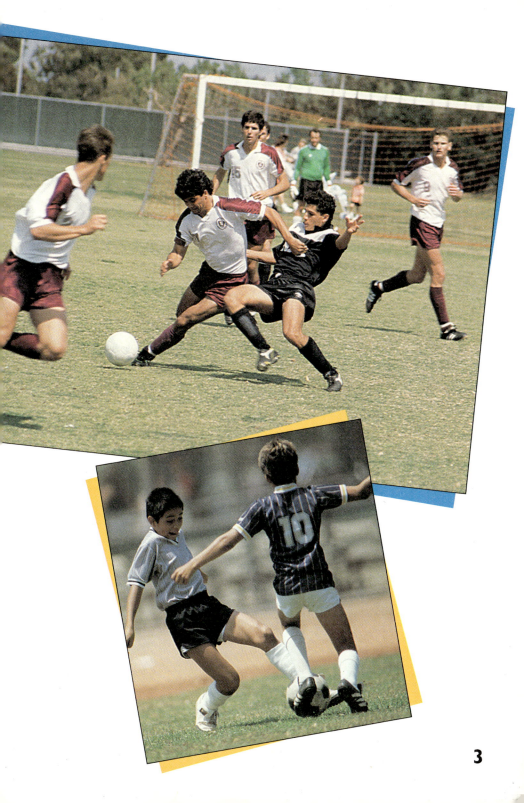

Millions of people around the world play soccer, including nearly 200 million kids in more than 100 countries. In 1995, two teams from Russia even played soccer at the North Pole. The temperature was 20 degrees below zero!

Americans have never been as excited about soccer as the rest of the world. The game has always been very important in Europe and South America, but has only recently become popular in the United States. Today, thousands of American children play soccer on organized teams or just for fun.

Where did soccer come from?

Soccer has been around a long time. Sports like it were played more than 2,000 years ago in Europe and Asia. Sometimes these games would have hundreds of people playing on fields that were several miles long.

Kicking games were also a favorite pastime in the days of knights and castles. In the year 1314, King Edward II of England banned the game. He felt too many people were playing instead of working! For 300 years it was against the law to play soccer.

In the late 1800s, British sailors spread the game throughout the world as they went from port to port. For a while, people called the game "association football." Then it was changed to "assoc," and then to "soccer."

How do you play?

The game may go by different names all over the world, but the rules are very much the same wherever soccer is played.

There is one main objective in soccer—to score goals. The team with the most goals wins the game. In international soccer, teams compete in 90-minute games. Each half is 45 minutes long. The clock stops only for a goal, a foul, or an injury. A foul often results in a free penalty kick for the other team.

Children often play soccer using three to seven players on a team. An international side has eleven players. The goal is guarded by the goalkeeper and defense players, who try to keep the ball out of the goal. The rest of the team is made up of midfielders, who roam the middle of the field, and forwards, who score most of the goals.

Soccer players usually wear colored jerseys, shorts, heavy socks, and cleated shoes. Unlike American football, soccer players do not wear pads or helmets.

What is the World Cup?

The World Cup is the most popular sporting event in the world. It is a month-long soccer tournament held every four years. National teams from all over the world compete.

The first World Cup took place in the South American country of Uruguay in 1930. Thirteen teams took part in the tournament. In 1994, more than 140 countries tried out for one of 24 spots in the World Cup finals.

The 1994 World Cup championship game between Brazil and Italy was watched on television by more than one billion people! Brazil won a record fourth World Cup trophy when Italian star Roberto Baggio missed a very important penalty kick at the end of the game.

Who is the best ever?

There have been many soccer superstars. They have come from all over the world, especially Europe and South America.

Peter Shilton
England

Michelle Akers
USA

Diego Maradona

Argentina

Franz Beckenbauer

Germany

Pele is the nickname of the man many people call the greatest soccer player ever. His real name is Edson Arantes do Nascimiento. Pele led Brazil to the World Cup championship in 1958, 1962, and 1970.

For almost 20 years, Pele played for a team in Brazil called the Santos. He scored 1,219 goals in 1,254 games. In 1975, he left Brazil to play for the New York Cosmos. He helped make soccer a popular sport in the United States.

Remember, you can play soccer almost anywhere. If you don't have a soccer ball, you can use some rolled up socks. If you don't have a goal, you can use a pair of trees or rocks or hats. Keep practicing, and you may become a star. You may become the next Michelle Akers or Roberto Baggio. Or even the next Pele!